A Chosen Generation

*How God Is Calling Young People
to a Higher Purpose*

Madeline Whitmore

Dedication

I dedicate this book to my incredible youth pastors, Asim and Lisa Trent. Your passion to see God move in this generation is unbelievably inspiring and absolutely contagious. Thank you for everything you have done for me and so many other young people. The Lord has amazing things in store for you and I can't wait to see it all happen.

"It is for freedom that Christ has set us free. Stand firm, then, and do not let yourselves be burdened again by a yoke of slavery" (Galatians 5:1).

Table of Contents

Part 1
First Things First

Part 2
Leave Yourself Behind

Part 3
Get in the Game

Desperation

I feel a great sense of desperation as I sit down to write this. I feel the Lord tugging on my heart and calling me to this generation, my generation, in order to make some kind of change. I am so tired of the school shootings, the suicides, and all of the various tragedies that happen every day but could be prevented. Maybe you feel as though the terrible things going on around you don't concern you, or perhaps you'd rather believe these things aren't happening because they're far too difficult to face. Maybe you even feel distant from God because it's hard to understand why He would let the awful things happen that you watch every night on the news.

Every time a tragedy happens I feel increasingly desperate to see God move and to see *something* change in our world. This time, though, I'm tired of sitting back in defeat, shaking my fists at the sky, and saying, "*Why,* God? *Why* do such horrible things have to happen?" I'm tired of going through my own vicious cycle of being angry and asking God to change the world, but immediately turning my attention back to myself until the next calamity comes. I don't just want to pray for comfort for victims after the fact; I want to pray for the prevention of tragedy. I want to see an outpouring of the Holy Spirit on this world that changes lives and breaks chains and rescues hearts from sin and from darkness. I want to see God move in a way that *changes* how things are and actually *does something* to fight against the evil and pain in our world.

I believe that no matter how old you are, you are called to leadership within the specific generation that you are part of. We are called to serve and transform the people of our generation, or in other words for us teenagers, the kids we're growing up with. On a larger scale, we are called to lead every person all around the world that is included in our own generation. As teenagers our job is especially important because we are the people who will be next to run the world, but do you honestly think we're prepared for that? Would our generation be able to guide the *entire world* through Christian leadership? Think about it.

So all that being said, I am desperate to see God move over this generation because I am tired of the apathetic attitude towards the growing evil in this world. I can no longer sit back and watch the world fall apart.

I'm ready to step up and be used by God. Who's with me?

INTRODUCTION

The Status of a Generation

Have you ever wondered if there's something in your life that you're missing or thought that there's something *more* to life than the way you're living it now? Maybe you sense that there's something going on that's *way* greater than yourself and you want to be a part of it. Well, I believe that there *is* something happening and I think that God is moving in the people of our generation. Seeing the things that God is doing makes me want to join in the movement. I don't want to miss a single second of what God has in store for us.

Let me back up for a minute. We are living at a crucial point in history. Our world is on the verge of either greatness or absolute destruction. I would even say that the next step relies on our generation and whether we choose to step up and be leaders or whether we remain complacent. The amount of God that's allowed in our lives is diminishing with every law that's passed. The government has put in place the separation of church and state, freedom from religion, censorship, and so many other things that try to make God *less* instead of *greater* in our lives. There are so many people who live every day hopelessly and live without the knowledge that their life has a purpose as the awful state of this world weighs on them. Pain is all around and it is absolutely everywhere you look; sorrow seems practically inescapable.

As Christians, though, we know differently. We understand that there is a loving God who has promised us life and a future. We believe in the saving power of our Lord Jesus Christ and we recognize the forgiveness of our sins. Think about the hope you first felt when you were saved and born again. There are millions of people who have never, and may never, know what it feels like to experience the type of love that reaches so deep that it can even change who you are. There are millions of people who walk around barely surviving because they've lost any will to live.

But how do we respond to the hurt that's all around us? We put "Christian" for our religious beliefs on our Facebook profiles and try not to do anything *too* bad that might make people think we aren't really Christians. We have no compassion for the lost or any passion to see people saved anymore. Unfortunately, this type of life that's lived halfway for Jesus is not the life we're called to live. By living in a way that doesn't completely profess Jesus as Lord, I can guarantee that we will never see any type of change in our world.

We get excited when we hear about revivals starting on school campuses amongst young people and want to be involved in the flare-ups, but once the initial passion starts to fade it's almost as though nothing even happened in the first place. With this unending cycle of hot and then cold, there will be no lasting transformation in anyone's life, which is the purpose of Christianity—*to be transformed by Christ and become more like Him.*

I believe that this hot and cold living describes the status of our generation. If something interests us we'll grab onto it as long as it can hold our attention but let it go as soon as it actually requires something of us or costs us something. Maybe you roll your eyes when your parents or grandparents make a negative comment about "this generation," but don't you think they have a point? We've been called apathetic, lazy, hopeless, you name it.

Look around at your friends' lives and even your own. How many people do you know who actually have ambition and daily pursue their goals? How many people do you see who continue to fight for a cause they are passionate about even after it's no longer headline news? I'm guessing that the answer is "not very many," and that's why I believe our generation is characterized by passionate outbursts followed by dry spells of complacency. We have a mentality that demands: "Entertain me," and if something doesn't hold our attention for more than five minutes we move on to the next thing that we think will fulfill us.

Another problem that I see within Christian teenagers is that actions don't mean anything anymore. Too many of us say we're "Christian," but our lives do not reflect Jesus in any way, shape, or form. We either don't know or don't care that we were created for a purpose and that we actually *can* do something meaningful with our lives. Many of us have no regard for the consequences of our actions and do whatever we can in order to make ourselves happy no matter what the cost. I say "we" and "our" because these negative qualities are things I struggle with every day just like everyone else.

Now, I realize that the last few paragraphs amount to a lot of criticism, but let me talk about the positives I see in our generation and why I believe the Lord has such huge things in store for us. First, this generation is *passionate.* I've never seen people rally around a cause more than the teenagers of this generation. If there's something that we're passionate about or something we want to see changed, teenagers are often the ones at the head of the movement.

Another thing is that we're all looking for something greater and we all want to be part of something bigger than ourselves. Kids aren't satisfied with simply living; they want something more and they sense that there's some secret our leaders aren't telling us. Teenagers today find joy and fulfillment in the knowledge that they are making a difference, and this is such an encouraging attribute.

Finally, we know how to use our resources because we are truly a generation of technology. Think about how easy it is for you to learn how to use a new phone or new laptop when it takes your parents and grandparents twice as long to figure them out. We grew up with new technology coming out constantly, so we know all about the power that it holds. At this time in history, all information is spread through the Internet, social media, and through the use of technology, so we know how to use that to our advantage to create a movement.

So that's what I believe is the status of our generation. We have a lot of great things about us, but also a lot of faults to overcome. If we turned the passion that characterizes our generation into a passion for serving God and a heart for His Kingdom, I believe we would see incredible change in our lives and in our world.

I know that our futures would be a lot brighter, and the kids after us would have a much better world to inherit. All of this is great to say and to dream about, but unless it is turned into action my words will mean nothing. I challenge you to keep reading in order to learn more about what I believe is a calling from the Lord on your life to stand up and be a leader in order to change the world.

PART 1

First Things First

CHAPTER 1

A Season of Seeking

I've been seriously following the Lord for about a year and a half, and although that isn't a long period of time, I've learned a lot about what it means to pursue God and to be a Christian. One of the biggest things that the Lord has taught me is that He takes us through "seasons" of our lives. A "season" of life is a time—whether it's a few weeks, months, or years—which God leads us through in order to grow more in our walk with Christ and to build a closer relationship with Him. Sometimes there are dry seasons where you may not feel a lot of God's presence in your life. Sometimes there are seasons of growth where you really feel God pushing you to be all that He knows you can be. Sometimes there are difficult seasons where you are forced to rely solely on God to bring you through.

Whatever type of season you face, it's always designed to help you become more Christlike and to grow closer to God. The Bible says that "There is a time for everything, and a season for every activity under the heavens" (Ecclesiastes 3:1), meaning that there is a very specific time that God brings things into our lives in order to help us learn more about Him. I don't believe that God is boring, so why would He want us to have a life that looks the same day in and day out? The different seasons of life are one of the most exciting things about Christianity.

For all of us, there is a season that God uses in our lives to learn how to pursue Him and it's one of the most important seasons we could have. Think about where your life was when you were saved or even where you are right now if you're just starting to follow the Lord. I would argue that most of us didn't have a life that was perfectly put together when we came to repentance at the cross, and if we're being honest, then we probably *still* don't have everything figured out. But God uses every moment of our lives, good or bad, to take us through different seasons, and sometimes you have to recognize that there is a season where "He says, 'Be still, and know that I am God'" (Psalm 46:10).

When we have a passion for the Lord and we want to do "big things" for God, we forget the importance of actually pursuing Him. Too often we say, "Okay God, if You want me to do something, You have to give me a sign and come to me," or, "I want to be important to Your Kingdom, Jesus, so bring me to the big things now!" But that isn't how following Him should go. Yes, God sometimes does call you out when you least expect it, but most of the time He wants us to know the joy of seeking Him before anything else can happen.

God is always pursuing us because that's who He is, but we get frustrated when we can't feel His presence in our lives. A relationship is a two-way street and God always puts in His side, so I would guess that when we face times of frustration, then we aren't pursuing the relationship on our end. How would a relationship between a husband and wife work if only one person was pursuing the relationship? Our walk with God is exactly the same way.

There are seasons of life when God doesn't want you to worry about performing in huge ways, but He simply wants you to pursue Him relentlessly. My life verse is Jeremiah 29:13 which says, "You will seek [M]e and find [M]e when you seek [M]e with all your heart" because it is an amazing reminder that if I want God in my life, I have to seek Him with all my heart. Did you catch that? God says *all* your heart. Not just *some* of your heart or *when you have time,* but *all* of your heart. The Lord desires every single part of us to pursue Him and seek Him. Not only is this verse encouraging because God says that we will find Him if we seek Him, but it's also one of His promises! God vowed that if we pursue Him, then we'll be able to have a relationship with Him.

Our generation has lost the passion for actually pursuing something for more than just a short amount of time. Frankly, we just want everything handed to us and aren't willing to work for it ourselves. This entitlement mind-set has translated into our relationship with God. We expect the God of the universe to come and serve us when He already *did* serve us by dying on the cross and making it possible to have a relationship with Him.

In the Old Testament, only the holiest people could go into the temple to meet with God. The rest of the people did not get to live with the knowledge that God was accessible because they were separated from Him by sin, just as we still are today. When Jesus died on the cross as a sin offering, the curtain that kept the holiest part of the temple where God's Spirit dwelt, separated from everything else, was "torn in two" (Luke 23:45), symbolizing that God was available to all people, not just the high priest, if we repent and leave our lives of sin that keep us from Him.

In Christianity today, we take it for granted that God is right in front of us to be pursued and we expect Him to continue to serve us by giving us a sign or having

Him come to us. The fact is that we were created to *serve*, not to *be served*, and humbling yourself to seek the Lord is an act of servitude that too many of us are unwilling to perform.

Part of our lack of pursuit may be a sense of fear that even if we seek God we won't find Him. If you seek God, you will find God because that is a promise He gives in His Word, and the Lord keeps all of His promises. The first time you get on your knees and ask God for the forgiveness of your sins or the first time you raise your hands in worship may not be the time that God speaks to you, but don't give up right then. The Lord wants to see that no matter what you *feel*, you will seek Him. He wants to see perseverance and patience in your heart as you wait on Him to come to you because He will reveal Himself at the perfect time.

In the times when you wonder where God is, He may be waiting for the right time to come to you in a way that fits in with His plan, so do not relent! If you base your knowledge of God on whether or not you can feel Him, you limit the greatness of our God to a flawed, human emotion. The Lord is not just the tears in your eyes when you raise your hands at a powerful time of worship or the goose bumps on your arms when your pastor says something impactful. God is *real*, and He is more than just a feeling.

Our generation needs to learn that we cannot put God on our own agendas. We cannot just seek Him when we feel like it or when the passion increases or when we see other people seeking Him. We cannot fall on our knees before Him only when we need Him. If we ever hope to be leaders, we need to be known as a generation that seeks the face of God in every situation no matter how we feel. We may be in the worst pit of our lives but we still have to pursue the relationship with God that He has called us into.

I am emphasizing this part of your relationship with God because my pastor always says that you have to be who you're supposed to be before you do what you're supposed to do. Seeking God *will* change you. Over time, you're going to become a different person after spending time actually pursuing God because the knowledge and presence of God is strong enough to make you a new person. God isn't going to use you for big things until He knows you're ready to be used.

The Lord can use absolutely anyone or anything He wants to accomplish His purposes, but He wants your heart to be in the right place first. So if you want God to use you but aren't willing to seek Him, take a step back and look at the motives of your heart, because your lack of desire for God may be the reason He hasn't used you yet.

Maybe after reading this and learning more about the importance of pursuing God, you'll be called into a season of seeking Him. Practically speaking, what does seeking God look like? Pursuing God is different for every person, but there are a few main things I believe you should be doing in order to better your walk with the Lord.

First and most important is that you need to read your Bible. The Bible is your *daily bread*, meaning that you cannot live without it. Be addicted to the Word of God because it is powerful. Hebrews 4:12 says, "For the word of God is alive and active. Sharper than any double-edged sword, it penetrates even to dividing soul and spirit, joints and marrow; it judges the thoughts and attitudes of the heart." If you dig into the Word and ask God to let it change you, it will.

By reading your Bible you will learn more about the Lord (and more about yourself), than anything or anyone else would be able to teach you. Get into the Word every day, even if that means only taking one verse at a time and really meditating on it. Whatever the Lord calls you to read will be the perfect amount for you.

Next, get involved in a church or a youth group. You need people to pour into your life when you are in a season of growth, and there's no better place to find Godly men and women than in the Church. All churches are run by flawed individuals, so no church will be perfect; but it is very important to surround yourself with Godly people and to have times of worship in order to connect with God. Never put *too* much of your trust in a church because your pastor and your leaders will never be perfect, and Jesus is the only person you should completely rely on in your walk with God.

Make sure the doctrinal beliefs and values of your church match up with what God actually says in the Bible, because there are a lot of churches out there that do not actually teach the truth, which is another reason why it's so important to read your Bible and know what the real truth is. Having a support system of other believers is crucial because God has called us into fellowship with one another and it's comforting to know that you have people on your side who believe the same things you do.

Finally, if you hope to pursue God and set yourself apart to let Him use you, you have to separate yourself from the things of this world that keep you from the Lord. In my own life, I have to be very careful about the music I listen to, the things I watch, and the things I do with my time because many things keep me separated from God. For example, if I listen to too much secular music or watch too much trash TV, I start to feel distant from God because the negativity really affects me!

Unfortunately, leaving the distractions of the world behind is something that keeps a lot of teenagers from reaching their full potential. You may feel like your life would be boring without worldly things or that you'll be missing out on something if you begin to give things up, but there are way better things to come than anything you leave behind. Once you start to pursue God more, the conviction of the Holy Spirit will show you things that keep you from a stronger relationship with the Lord and you may feel the need to let the old things go. When you come to a crossroads between holding onto something and letting it go, think about where you really want your heart to be and the fulfillment that comes from knowing God. If you have to give something up, remember that the Lord's presence is more fulfilling than anything else in this world.

Another thing I've learned from experiencing different seasons in my walk with Christ is that sometimes I really don't feel like seeking God. I either feel lazy because I don't want to put in the work or even discouraged because it seems like I'll never be able to be close to God. God has shown me that everything, even repentance, is a gift He gives us. Even a passion for the Lord and a fire to pursue Him is His doing, not ours. We cannot muster up the desire to seek God on our own because it just isn't natural. Our sinful nature wants to keep us separated from God; it doesn't encourage us to seek Him, to say the least.

Though it shouldn't matter what you *feel* when you decide to follow God, because God is more than a feeling, you *can* pray for a fire for the Lord. The prophet Elijah prayed that God would send literal fire from Heaven on his altar so that the people would know that God is the one true God, and God answered. Just as fire fell from Heaven on Elijah's altar, fire for the Lord can also fill your life. Are you willing to wait on the Lord? Are you willing to serve God while you are waiting for Him to reveal Himself to you?

Sometimes the Lord wants to teach us about pursuing Him even when we don't feel any passion, but praying for more fire for the Lord is something we should always be doing. If you feel discouraged or condemned because you don't have any desire to pursue the Lord, ask God to rain life on your spirit. He may hold back the rain to teach you something, but He'll open the floodgates of Heaven when the soil of your heart is ready.

The seasons of life where we really pursue God are exciting, but always remember that no matter what season God is bringing you through, you always need to be seeking the Lord because that is what sets us apart from all other people. Christians are different from the world because we do not live as the world does. We have been called to something greater, so we have to do things differently than everyone else. If your life does not look any different from a person of the world, can you really say that you are following Jesus? If you hope to be used by God in big ways, seeking Him and being faithful in the little things are where you need to start. Find God, know who He is, and learn who you are first. When you make a conscious decision that you want God to use you, He probably won't call you into a huge role right away. Make sure that you are faithfully pursuing God first, and over time He will begin to lead you into bigger and bigger things. We need a generation of teenagers who seek God in order to be able to make a difference in our world. There is so much power in the name of Jesus that if we learn to seek the Lord with all we have and He begins to change us, we will be unstoppable.

"Sow righteousness for yourselves, reap the fruit of unfailing love, and break up your unplowed ground; for it is time to seek the Lord, until he comes and showers his righteousness on you" (Hosea 10:12).

CHAPTER 2

Utter Dependence

D o you know that we cannot do anything good without God? It's impossible to act in a way that's Christlike without God's help. Even though we have the Spirit of God living inside of us, our sinful flesh that surrounds the Spirit is still strong. In his letter to the Romans, the author Paul says, "For I know that good itself does not dwell in me, that is, in my sinful nature. For I have the desire to do what is good, but I cannot carry it out" (Romans 7:18).

You may have felt the struggle that most Christians face every day—you want to "be good" and do "good things"—but it seems impossible because you just keep messing up! No matter how hard you try, you always fail and you think you'll never be able to break the cycle. Maybe you even keep a tally of all the times you mess up and you relive your mistakes constantly. You may have some "good" days where you don't do anything really bad, but most of the time you just keep failing.

If you feel like I just described your relationship with Jesus, then you aren't alone. Coming to the point of realizing that no matter how hard you try, you'll never be good enough on your own is crucial in your walk with God. We have to let go of trying to do everything by ourselves because self-reliance does not work. You can try all you want to change the world by yourself, but absolutely nothing will get done. A movement attempted by our own power and strength will not prevail, but a movement by the hand of God will be unstoppable.

In the book of Acts, the apostles were called to evangelize to the nations and were persecuted in the process. In one instance, some of the apostles were brought before the Sanhedrin, who were a type of court of Israel, to be questioned by the high priest because they were teaching the people about Jesus when they were specifically told not to do so. The whole Sanhedrin wanted to put the apostles to death, but a man of the court named Gamaliel reminded the other leaders of all the movements that people had started in the past and how their progress quickly fell apart after their leader was killed. Because Jesus had just been crucified, Gamaliel probably assumed that the apostles would eventually give up when he said, "Therefore, in the present case I advise you: Leave these men alone! Let them go! For if their purpose or activity is of human origin, it will fail. But if it is from God, you will not be able to stop these men; you will only find yourselves fighting against God" (Acts 5:38-39). Wow! This is one of my favorite passages of Scripture because it is another reminder of God's great power. With God in control as we rise up to claim this generation for His glory, nothing will be able to stop us.

The problem is that it's difficult to give up control and let God take over. It's much easier to work for something on our own because it's scary to have faith and give our dreams over to the Lord. Just as it is true that there won't be any change in our generation without God's help, it's also true that there won't be any change in our own lives without the Lord's intervention. We have to get to the end of ourselves and realize that we cannot live our lives on our own because we need God to be in control. When we let God be the Lord of our lives, we give Him the chance to change us from the inside out. Changed people are what is going to change our generation.

In order to make any progress in your own life, you have to realize how utterly depraved and insufficient we are as human beings. Without God intervening in our lives, we are completely lost. We are called to love our neighbor, but we can't even *love* without God's help because the ability to love isn't in our sinful nature. We cannot stand up against any temptation that the world throws at us because we are far too weak. Left to our own power, we won't be able to tell anyone about Jesus, represent Jesus to the world, or even serve Jesus.

You can do all the great and noble things that you want, but if they're done in your own power and for the wrong reasons it means nothing. It isn't enough to just be a "good person" who usually doesn't break any of the Ten Commandments; we have to be people who are so changed by God that it's obvious we aren't acting in our own power. If I haven't gotten the point across enough I'll say it again: We cannot do anything without God. If we want to see anything in our world change, we need to be a generation of people who are completely dependent on Him.

Be radically, utterly, unchangeably dependent on Jesus Christ and realize that you cannot live without Him. He is everything. God wants to see a generation who is so dependent on Him that we know we cannot change the world without His mighty help. The Lord longs to show His power and might to His people; we just need to give Him a chance to do so by stepping out of our own way and letting Him take over. The

Bible says that "the eyes of the Lord range throughout the earth to strengthen those whose hearts are fully committed to him" (2 Chronicles 16:9), meaning that God is waiting for our move. He is waiting for us to cry out to Him.

Once you realize that you are incredibly dependent on Jesus, that's when an *exchange of life* begins to occur. When you lay down your life, Jesus will then take it and give you His instead. When you pick up your cross in order to follow Jesus, He will begin to change the deepest parts of your nature into something beautiful that He can use for His glory. We need a generation of people who are willing to give up control of their own lives in exchange for Jesus' life. When this exchange occurs, God will begin to do a work in the hearts of His people and a movement by the power of God will be unstoppable.

If living in a way that depends completely on the Lord seems too difficult or scary for you, then you're on the right track and you're coming to the end of yourself. Frankly, you're even going to need God's help to *realize* you need His help. When you recognize that your life is nothing, but Christ in you is everything, that is the definition of repentance and that is how you get your life right with Jesus.

True repentance isn't just reciting a prayer that says you believe Jesus died for you. True repentance is turning from the life of sin you once knew and leaving it far behind. The word "repent" frightens people and has gained a negative connotation, but the word that is used for "repent" in the Bible means to "change one's mind for the better." Repentance means changing your mind to lay down the life of darkness you once knew and stepping into the light that Jesus has for you. Repentance doesn't have to be a big deal either, like where you come down to the altar at a church service. Getting on your knees in your bedroom and declaring before the Lord that you don't want to live a life of sin anymore is just as powerful as an altar call.

Finding God first is an essential step in seeing God move in our generation. If we want to see change in our generation, we need to get back to the true meaning of repentance, which is turning your life around, coming back to Jesus, and realizing how badly you need Him. We must be utterly dependent on God because without Him we can do nothing. Let God take your life. You're still going to mess up and you're still going to fail because you're human. You'll say the wrong thing when you're trying to tell someone about your faith or do something that isn't Christlike, but that's okay.

Often people can only see your actions and they judge based on what is visible, but God sees your heart behind what you do. He understands that you're only human and He knows the motivations of your heart.

Jesus looks on you with so much love. Rely on the grace and mercy of God to change you and don't sweat the small stuff. If your heart is sincere in seeking Him but you mess up along the way, God understands. He just wants you to get back up and try again.

So seek the Lord as though your life depends on it, because it really does. Lean on God and trust that He will support you in every way. Come to the place where you are so dependent on Jesus that the thought of even going one minute without Him seems impossible. Never believe that you're weak because you need to rely so much on God; the strongest people are the ones who aren't in control of their own lives.

CHAPTER 3

Unleashing the Holy Spirit

God is not just God the Father and God the Son; He is also God the Holy Spirit. We know that God is our Heavenly Father who is all powerful and we know that God came to earth in the form of the man Jesus, but do we understand who the Holy Spirit is? I believe that the Holy Spirit is the most forgotten member of the Trinity, which is incredibly dangerous. If I were Satan, our greatest enemy who wants to keep us from the Lord, I would most want God's people to forget that they had the power of the Spirit living inside of them because without it they wouldn't be any threat to the devil and his kingdom.

The Holy Spirit is God's presence living inside each of His followers. Because the Spirit is a member of the Trinity, He is fully God. This means that *all of God lives inside of us.* The Bible says that "the Spirit of [H]im who raised Jesus from the dead is living in you" (Romans 8:11). This means that in you, you have the power to heal the sick, give sight to the blind, see the lame walk, and raise the dead to life. Yet we live every single day without the knowledge of the power that God gives us to show Himself to the world!

If God's people do not take advantage of the Holy Spirit, we are powerless. Without unleashing the Holy Spirit inside of us, we won't see any change in ourselves or those around us. Not only does the Spirit perform miraculous wonders, but He is also the quiet whisper to encourage you in a time of need. He's the words you're given when you're trying to evangelize but don't know what to say. He's the strength to help you overcome an addiction that you just can't seem to break. He's the impossible peace that you feel when it seems to the rest of the world that you should be falling apart. The Holy Spirit is everything you need.

It is the Holy Spirit who moves in people's hearts to bring them to Jesus, so no one can even know God without Him. The Holy Spirit is also the light of Jesus that other people see when they notice that something's different about you, which is why taking advantage of Him is crucial. Jesus told us in His Sermon on the Mount about a light that can't be hidden, and that light is the Holy Spirit inside of you. When you start to unleash the power of the Holy Spirit in your life, people *will* notice—especially if you've never relied on Him before. People will be drawn to the light that is inside of you, even if they don't know that it's the Holy Spirit who reels them in. You cannot change yourself to be a "better" person; you have to rely on the Holy Spirit to make you more and more Christlike. Just like I said earlier, you cannot do anything good without God and you won't become someone God can use by just trying harder.

So how do we start to experience more of the Holy Spirit in our lives? First, recognize He's there. The Spirit is in you at all times and in all situations. He is always with you. You are never without God because He lives inside of you. If you're facing temptation, the Spirit is just waiting for you to call on Him for strength. He helps you day in and day out without you even realizing it.

Next, pray for more of the Spirit. All of God lives inside of you, so you aren't praying for God to increase Himself. When you ask for more of the Spirit, you're asking to be able to experience more of God in your life. He's already completely there; we just have to get ourselves out of the way to be able to recognize that He is. In the mornings when you wake up, ask the Holy Spirit to come and fill you up. Ask Him to fill you with the fruits of the Spirit—love, joy, peace, patience, kindness, goodness, faithfulness, gentleness, self-control—in order to be able to show Christ's love to the world. If there's something specific you're struggling with in your certain season of life, ask the Holy Spirit to give you strength to face the day. No matter how silly it may sound, you can ask the Spirit for anything. Because the Spirit is God Himself, He longs to give you good gifts just like the Father does.

Relying on the Holy Spirit to live your life for you is a freeing process because you give up control of your life into the hands of an almighty God. The problem with unleashing the Holy Spirit in your life is that you become a threat to stop the works of the devil and the enemy definitely doesn't like that. Satan might try to put fear in your life to hold you back. You may begin to be fearful of letting the Spirit enter you because He might lead you into doing something that's outside of your comfort zone. I face the fear of completely letting the Holy Spirit work through me every day because I worry that the Lord is going to lead me to do something that scares me.

When we face those moments of fear, we have to remember that fear is of the enemy. The Bible says that "perfect love [the love of God] drives out fear" (1 John 4:18), and, "For the Spirit God gave us does not makes us timid, but gives us power, love and self-discipline" (2 Timothy 1:7). Courage and boldness are also traits that come through the power of the Holy

Spirit, and when you feel any fear at all, ask God to give you bravery. A life lived without the Holy Spirit may be safe, but it will also be a life filled with regrets and missed opportunities.

When you begin to let the Holy Spirit change you, people are going to notice. In the book of Acts, the apostles Peter and John were called before the Sanhedrin and they spoke the Word of God fearlessly in front of men who wanted to kill them. The Bible says that, "When they [the Sanhedrin] saw the courage of Peter and John and realized that they were unschooled, ordinary men, they were astonished and they took note that these men had been with Jesus" (Acts 4:13).

You don't have to go to a seminary to become a pastor or study theology for years to make it obvious that you follow Jesus. It says Peter and John were ordinary people, but everyone knew that they followed the Lord. If you start to unleash the power of the Spirit in your life, people will see Jesus even if they don't know that's who they're looking at. Your life is a testimony to what or to whom you follow, so make your life evidence of Someone who's actually worth following.

Don't be afraid to let the Spirit lead you and change you. If you let Him, the Spirit will cleanse you of everything that isn't pleasing to Him. Sometimes the cleansing process will be like pulling teeth and it'll be painful, especially if there is sin in your life that you've held onto for years. But I've found that those seasons where God points out the junk in your heart and says that He wants to remove it are truly the most exciting times of life. I cannot stress enough that people are going to notice that you are a changed person.

You might be a Paul, who was somebody that persecuted Christians and admitted that he was the worst of all sinners until he was radically saved by Jesus and started to do huge things for God. Maybe you're a Peter, who faithfully followed Jesus but had moments of doubt, fear, and denial until he received the Holy Spirit and spoke boldly to thousands about the saving power of the cross. The possibilities are endless, but you have to be willing to be radically changed by the power of the Holy Spirit or none of God's promises will actually come to pass.

If you want to see change in your generation, the change must first come in yourself. One sinner who is radically saved and begins to boldly proclaim the name of Jesus could change the world, so what if you're that person? That's what the Holy Spirit can do.

CHAPTER 4

You're Hot and You're Cold

I mentioned earlier that I believe the "hot and cold" mentality is one that defines our generation. We latch ourselves onto something when it's popular or when it's right in front of us, but we let it go the very next minute. Things go in and out of style all the time, and unfortunately, many people view their relationship with God as something that's only a passing trend. Maybe you see Jesus as the "back pocket" God who you can pull out to rely on when you're really in trouble. Maybe you treat God as your "cosmic genie" who you only talk to when there's something that you want. Maybe you only say you're a Christian because your family or your friends would freak out if you told them you weren't really sure what you believe. Whatever it is, we first need to establish where God's heart really is and what He expects from us as His followers.

When Jesus is speaking to the Laodicean church in the book of Revelation, He says, "I know your deeds, that you are neither cold nor hot. I wish you were either one or the other! So, because you are lukewarm—neither hot nor cold—I am about to spit you out of my mouth" (Revelation 3:15-16). Though there are a lot of different opinions as to what this verse means, I believe Jesus is saying that He wants His people to be fully committed to Him. "Cold" is the state of not knowing Jesus or even turning against Him; "hot" is the state of being dedicated to the Lord and knowing that you stand for Him; and "lukewarm" is the awkward in-between of only loving Jesus sometimes or changing your mind about Him being the Lord of your life.

Another good definition of "lukewarm" that I've learned from personal experience is saying that you're a Christian but not living in a way that reflects your faith. When we look at this verse, it's obvious that Jesus doesn't want to see a life that is lived only halfway; that isn't even tolerable to Him! Basically, Jesus is telling us that He wishes we would just make up our minds and take a stand for something—not just have one foot in and one foot out.

Many times people take the word "hot" and assume it means you have to be a Charismatic Christian who jumps up and down in church and who lives a "perfect" Christian life, but that isn't what Jesus is asking. First of all, we're all made to follow Jesus in ways that are unique to each of us individually, so if you aren't someone who's a loud worshipper, that's completely okay. Second, Jesus isn't asking us to always be perfect. Just because you've decided to fix your eyes on Jesus doesn't mean that every day in your walk with God is going to go well. Because we're flawed people, our passion for God ebbs and flows throughout our whole lives and He understands that.

This verse in Revelation is trying to show that God wants His people to be firmly committed to Him and to have their hearts set on Him no matter how they *feel*. He wants us to know who we believe in and why we believe in Him. He wants a people who will stand firm and won't be shaken by the storms of life. Even when we fail we need to get back up and keep pressing on towards Jesus. Most importantly, God wants to know that we won't seek Him only when we feel His presence, but all the time, because He isn't just an emotion.

We cannot live lukewarm lives anymore. This generation needs to be hot if we ever want to see anything change. I'm really tired of seeing people say that they follow Jesus, but in reality the term "Christian" is just a title to them. We cannot say that we're Christians and continue to live a life of sin. Sin and Christ do not go together. Yes, we are still going to sin when we try to follow Jesus, but we have to make a conscious effort to focus more on Jesus so that we begin to sin less. Many times when Jesus healed people, He told them to "go and sin no more" or to "leave your life of sin." Obviously He understood that the people were never going to be perfect, but He wanted to see that their hearts would turn to Him instead of to sin.

No more lukewarm. No more following Jesus when it's easy but abandoning Him when it costs us something. No more of mentioning His name once in a while on our Facebook statuses or only thinking about Him on Sundays. Jesus wants us to be all in for the ride. This generation needs to stop our wavering and start our commitment. When we choose to leave mediocrity behind, people are going to notice that we're living extraordinary lives, and who knows? Maybe they'll even want to try it for themselves to see what we have that they don't.

Actions

I hate to be harsh, but just because we say we're Christian doesn't actually mean that we are. Part of lukewarm living is having a mouth that says Jesus is Lord, but not having a life that declares the same. Take a minute to think about your life. What is it that you think about? What do you do on the weekends and in your free time? How do you spend your money? How do you treat other people? These are crucial questions that we need to start asking ourselves in order to see what message our lives are really giving.

I think part of the reason that the word "Christian" has such a negative connotation these days is because so many of us are just plain hypocritical. We use our mouths to say that we love Jesus but then cuss up a storm with our next breath. I often wonder if someone has looked at my life and thought, "and *that* is why I'm not a Christian." I hope that's as convicting to you as it is to me!

In his letter to the Romans, Paul is calling out the hypocrites of the time and he asks things such as, "You who say that people should not commit adultery, do you commit adultery?" (Romans 2:22), in regard to the Jews being an example to the Gentiles (which means anyone who isn't Jewish). He then he goes a step further to quote something the prophet Isaiah said when he tells the Jews, "'God's name is blasphemed among the Gentiles because of you'" (Romans 2:24). Putting this into terms that make sense for us Christians today, the question is, "Do nonbelievers talk badly against God because of the way you live?" Another quote I've heard says, "If you were put on trial for being a Christian, would there be enough evidence to convict you?" I sure hope there would be.

Who you *really* are is just as powerful, if not more important, as who you *claim* to be. The world has enough teenagers who say that they're Christian but have absolutely no regard for Christ. Choose to be different. If you bear the name Christian, you have a big responsibility. Refuse to conform to the way the rest of the world lives, because Christians are called to take a stand against the world. Yes, you are still going to fail because you aren't perfect, nor do you have to be. I keep stressing this point because it is so important to understand! Jesus absolutely does not expect you to live a perfect life. We need to have more Christians who humbly admit that they are sinners as the reason why they know they need a Savior, because the type of life that is surrendered to Jesus attracts people to His love.

Live differently than other people do. Go to church instead of sleeping in on Sunday. Listen to Christian music more often than secular music. Listen to podcasts and sermons of a lot of different pastors to receive extra wisdom. Love people instead of gossiping about them. Go out of your way to be kind to others. Respect all of the people in authority over you—your parents, teachers, coaches, law enforcement, etc.— because that isn't what's "cool" for a lot of teenagers. Stay home on your Friday and Saturday nights if the only other option you have is partying, or perhaps go to a youth group. Keep away from things such as music, movies, or TV shows that have a lot of sexual content. Read your Bible when you wake up in the morning or before you go to bed.

The list of things you can do to separate yourself from the world is endless. Don't see these examples of things you *have* to do to be a "good" Christian. Do them with a sincere heart because you know it will help you grow in your relationship with God. This doesn't mean you have to live under a rock without any contact from the world. My pastor says that as Christians we are insulated from the world, not isolated from it. By living *in* the world and not *of* it, people will see Christ in you.

In the book of Ephesians, Paul urges us to "live a life worthy of the calling you have received" (Ephesians 4:1). You have a high calling on your life. No matter how many times you've heard it before, God has a huge plan for you and He has incredibly great things in store, so live in a way that represents that holy calling! The way you live could be the reason someone turns to Christ. You never know who's watching to see why you act differently than the world does.

Having higher standards makes people take notice, and that is exactly what you want. When people know that you're a Christian, it is inevitable that they'll look at you differently, and that is a perfect opportunity to show people what it really means to follow Jesus. Use those opportunities to show the people the hope that you have, all because of the saving power of Jesus. Show Christ's love to others so that they'll see Him when they look at you. People are going to be watching anyway, so why not show them something that is worth their while?

Have you noticed a theme throughout Part One? If I broke all of it down into just a few last thoughts, Part One was about your own walk with God. Your heart has to be in the right place in order for God to use you to change the world. My prayer is that the Lord begins to awaken individuals and sets them ablaze for His glory because that would be the definition of a revival. All of the different parts of your walk with God can come down to one thing: seeking Him. If you truly, sincerely pursue God, all of what I described will begin to happen in your life. You'll become more dependent on Him, you'll see more of the Holy Spirit in your life, you'll be firmly committed to Jesus, and your actions will set you apart from everyone else. All it'll take to see some change in our generation is a few individuals who have a passion to see God move. Are you one of those people?

PART 2

Leave Yourself Behind

CHAPTER 5

Prayer

Prayer is powerful, and it should be your first response to any situation in life, good or bad. Prayer changes things, and prayer is where all possibilities begin. Besides having the Holy Spirit in us, prayer is the most effective weapon that we have in order to see change in our world. Why would we expect God to do anything about the evil in the world if He didn't know that we actually wanted Him to?

Prayer isn't necessarily faith in the thing we're praying *for*, but it's faith in the Person we're praying *to*. We need a generation of people who know how to pray bold prayers. Because of what Jesus did for us on the cross, we can come shamelessly to God's throne and ask for what we need. God promises that, "you may ask me for anything in my name, and I will do it" (John

14:14). Our generation needs to learn how to pray because "the prayer of a righteous person is powerful and effective" (James 5:16).

We need to learn that prayer isn't just a matter of asking God to grant our wishes. Prayer means to connect with God in order to learn more about *His* desires for us rather than just what *we* want. Learn to ask according to God's will. I heard a quote once that said, "God loves us too much to give us everything we want." Think about this for just a minute. What would your life be like if God gave you every single thing that you've ever asked for? Really think about this, because you might just say that life would be perfect! Look back on the blessings that God has given you and think about what would've happened if your own desires had gotten in the way. God loves you too much to give you anything that would hinder His perfect plan for your life, so we have to pray for *God's* will to be done, not *ours*.

Without asking God for anything, though, we'll never learn how to pray. If you never ask God for anything, you'll never learn what desires come from your own heart and what desires are actually God's. So ask! Ask for things that seem crazy. Ask that God would save someone you don't even know. Ask God to open doors for you to do important things for His Kingdom. Pray boldly because it gives God a chance to show

His power. The more you pray, the less selfish your desires will be and the more they will match up with what God wants. Never be afraid to ask God for something because you never know what could happen. The craziest prayer could change the world. If you don't ask, you'll never receive, so don't leave the gifts that God gives you unwrapped.

When you approach God in prayer remember to, "Enter [H]is gates with thanksgiving and [H]is courts with praise; give thanks to [H]im and praise [H]is name" (Psalm 100:4). Pray with a grateful heart that recognizes the goodness of God and all the blessings He pours out on you. Don't make your prayer life just about what *you* need; make sure to praise God and tell Him how great He is too.

Not only does prayer consist of presenting your needs before God, but it's also a way to spend time with Him. What do you do when you want to get to know someone better? You sit down with them and have a conversation! Prayer is simply having a conversation with God. The key word here is *conversation*, because a conversation involves two people, not just a one-person monolog. There are things you need to talk to God about, but there are also things that He wants to tell *you*, so make sure you spend time listening to Him along with talking to Him.

Sometimes being open and honest before the Lord is frightening, but God wants transparency from you. Just come to Him completely as you are; you don't have to put on any type of show. Talk to God the way you would talk to a close friend, because that's your most natural state. The more time you spend talking with Jesus, the more comfortable you'll feel and the better you'll know Him. By having more time in God's presence, you'll start to become more like Him, and becoming more Christlike is our main goal in Christianity. So pray *a lot*.

Do you know who the people are that pray the most? Desperate people. Desperate people pray because they don't have any other choice but to rely on God. Even people who don't believe in God might get down on their knees if they really need help. Whatever you believe about the world, I think we can all agree that we're in a pretty desperate situation with all the evil that happens around us, which makes this the perfect time for God to come in. Revivals don't start on their own; they start by prayer. Be desperate to see people saved. Be desperate to win your school for Christ. Be desperate to see your friends and family love Jesus. Be desperate to see change in yourself. We need to pray *fervently* and *relentlessly*, and desperate situations lend themselves to becoming the best times of prayer.

Think about who and what matters most to you in your life. Do you pray excessively for the most important parts of your life? Saturate yourself, those you love (and everyone else for that matter), the things you're passionate about, your dreams, and everything you can think of—with prayer. You can never pray *too much*. If you feel like you have no passion for anything, pray for passion too! By learning how to pray, God is going to begin to stir a fire in your heart that you won't be able to contain.

Prayer is something that is outside of yourself and something that is bigger than you are, so that's why I am emphasizing it so greatly. We first need to get our lives right with Jesus, but the next step after that is *action*. Before we can take any action, though, we need to *pray*. Prayer gives us the guidance and instruction we need in order to find out what God wants us to do. How can you expect God to tell you to go anywhere if you're never around to listen to Him?

I don't think that God wants wishy-washy prayers. I think God wants us to pray prayers that are bold. Little prayers are typically prayed when we don't have the amount of faith to believe that God is going to do what He promised. Jesus said, "Truly I tell you, if you have faith as small as a mustard seed, you can say to this mountain, 'Move from here to there', and it will move. Nothing will be impossible for you" (Matthew 17:20).

Do you know how small a mustard seed is? It's one of the smallest seeds in the world, but even with that small amount of faith Jesus says that nothing is impossible! Have so much faith in God that it seems stupid to other people. If you present a request before God but don't have faith that He'll answer you, why even ask in the first place? When you ask God for something, really ask Him for it. Don't be on the fence about anything. If you need a miracle, boldly ask for a miracle! Say, "Jesus, help me!" rather than "Jesus, would You maybe please show up just a little bit? Because that would be kind of helpful right now."

Don't get me wrong; humility is essential, and I'm not encouraging you to come arrogantly and demandingly to God's throne. What I'm saying is that we need to pray boldly with confidence and without fear that God might not answer our prayers. God answers any prayer, even prayers you didn't know you said, that are in His name and according to His will, and that's a promise. You have nothing to be afraid of, because even if God doesn't give you exactly what you thought you wanted, it's only because He's got something way better in mind.

Not only do we need to be bold, but we also need to be persistent. Jesus told a parable about a widow who kept going to the town judge for help. The judge would never help the woman but she still went back to him over and over until he finally gave in and helped her. The Bible says that Jesus told this story to His disciples to "show them that they should always pray and not give up" (Luke 18:1). What I take from this story is that the judge represents God and the woman represents desperate people like us. Now, God isn't mean or unsympathetic like the judge in the story, so how much more will God answer our prayers if we're persistent and keep on asking? Be persistent. Keep asking God. Yes, He did hear you the first time and He heard you before you even asked Him; but the Lord wants to see that we persevere and saturate our needs in prayer to show how much we desire Him. Always pray and never give up.

The more you pray, the more God will show you what to pray for. The list of prayer requests in this world is endless. You don't only have to pray for the people you know or for the things going on around you. Pray huge prayers that don't even make sense to you! Pray that you would *learn* how to pray. If you've started to feel a sense of desperation for our generation but you don't know what to do, please pray. Prayer may seem useless or futile, but prayer shakes the gates of Heaven.

We need a generation who prays over itself and asks for change. The Bible says to "pray continually" (1 Thessalonians 5:17), so pray all the time. If you don't know what to pray for, just pray for a move of God!

I cannot stress how important prayer is in any and all situations, no matter how big or small the circumstance may be. Even if you feel like there's absolutely nothing you can do to help our generation (which isn't true, by the way), then wage the prayer war.

Need some ideas of where to start?

Pray for yourself, that God would always be doing a work in you so that people would see more of Him. Pray that God would put huge dreams in your heart. Pray that He would make those dreams become a reality. You can dream huge dreams, because we have a huge God. Pray for protection over the calling God has placed on your life. Pray against the enemy and what he tries to do in people's lives to stop God from moving. Pray in the power of Jesus' name that the devil would stop messing with people. Pray for the people around you to support you and guide you as you navigate your way through being a Christian teenager. Pray for this generation, that God would rain His Spirit on us so that we would rise up as leaders. Pray for our world, that God would move because we are desperate for Him.

Pray boldly. Pray fearlessly. Always pray in the name of Jesus and by the power of Jesus.

My prayer for you is that you would become an absolute prayer warrior, because that is what we are all called to be.

CHAPTER 6

Unity

Let's say that you're going to play in a football game by yourself, meaning that you're the only person on your team. The team you're playing against has a different player for each position and they work well together. Each person on the other team only has to focus on their specific position and just do their best at what they're supposed to do. Since you're by yourself, you have to hike the ball, receive the ball, throw the ball, and then catch it a few yards down the field, completely by yourself. How well do you think that would work? You'd probably lose because there's no one else to help you. You'd never even think of playing sports by yourself, so why would you want to go through life by yourself? Yes, God is powerful enough to change the world through one person, but He didn't design us to have to do things on our own. Would you want to take on the weight of changing a generation by yourself?

God created everyone uniquely and with different talents, and we're called to use our talents in order to serve Him. All of us Christians together make up the body of Christ; we are His Church. "Just as a body, though one, has many parts, but all its many parts form one body, so it is with Christ" (1 Corinthians 12:12). Every person is a part of Christ's body and has their own special job, but every part works together to make the body function as a whole.

Think about if one day your pinky toe decided that it wasn't important to the body, so it removed itself from your foot. You wouldn't be able to walk the same and you'd be off-balance even without your littlest toe! Maybe you're feeling like the pinky toe of the body of Christ because you don't believe that you have any special talents to contribute to the Church. You were created with a purpose even if God hasn't revealed to you what that purpose is yet. You aren't going to stop being part of the body just because you don't feel as important! You are marked as a part of Christ's Church and you have a calling that only you can fulfill, so take heart.

God has placed responsibilities and opportunities in your life that only you can accomplish because only you have your specific set of talents and gifts. Whether or not you've come to the roles the Lord has called you to yet, there is still so much more ahead of you and no other person will be able to fulfill those roles as well as you can. I find comfort in the fact that I don't have to feel pressure to *do everything*, but that I can only be excellent in the things that God has called me to. Find out what talents the Lord has blessed you with and learn how to use them for His Kingdom.

You'll probably have to try a lot of different things before you find out what you're best at, so do new things! Also, don't feel like you *have* to do something specifically in the church, like being a pastor or a worship leader. The world needs Christian doctors, teachers, lawyers, construction workers, salespeople, and every other type of profession too! You can bring glory to God whether you're a pastor, a stay-at-home mom, a professional athlete, or a CEO. Find the place where you bring God the most glory and you'll be right in your wheelhouse.

If you find something you love to do and through it you bring glory to God, work at it with all your heart. The Bible says that "whatever you do, whether in word or deed, do it all in the name of the Lord Jesus, giving thanks to God the Father through him" (Colossians 3:17). Strive to be the best at your talent that you can be. The world has enough people who try to barely get by and do the least amount of work possible, so trying for excellence will be a great way to show Christ's light to the world.

If you're in the place you're supposed to be, doing what you're supposed to do, you *are* contributing to the body of Christ. When we all work together to bring glory to God, we can feel content that we are united in our efforts. The eyes do what the eyes are made to do and they don't worry about trying to be like the hands, but all together the body still works the way it's supposed to.

Use your talents to contribute to God's Kingdom in the way that you were made to contribute. If we want to see change in our generation, we have to be united. Even as we each do our specific jobs, we will still be united by the fact that we are all working towards a common goal of bringing glory to God. Even though every body part does only what it was made to do, each part works for the purpose of making the entire body thrive.

As a generation of young people, we have to find a common purpose. Individually and as a whole, our most important goal is to bring glory to God through everything we do and make His name famous in the world, but we are also called to our generation. We are called to rise up as leaders to fight against the evil that has completely filled the world. We are called to have a passion to see our generation become a people who seek God's face. If you don't know what your purpose is, just start learning how to live in a way that brings glory to God, and start to serve your generation in whatever way you can. Whether you want to serve at your church, start campus ministries at your school, or go on mission trips, you can serve the people of our generation and show them what it means to follow Jesus.

One of my favorite songs that inspires the Church to stand up for the Lord's purposes is called "We Will" by The Life Church Worship. The song talks a lot about the body of Christ going out into the world and showing Jesus' light. The song goes, "Consume us with Your kingdom's cause and we will shine where darkness falls... Nothing can stop Your church when we are one. Unified, we will show the world Your love... We will be the church and rise" (The Life Church). The words of this song have become the prayer that I have for our generation. I pray that we would rise up and have hearts that are set on fire for His Kingdom's cause. I pray that nothing would be able to stop us because we are unified.

We have to stand together and support each other as a generation. There are too many forces in the world that want to separate us and bring us down, but if we band together then no evil will be able to overtake the power of God in us. We are way stronger together than we are apart, so find other people who have the same passion for our generation as you do. If you don't know anyone who feels called to this generation, tell them about your passion and tell them why they're called to this generation too! Be the person who spreads unity among believers so that we can show the world that we are followers of Jesus.

When Jesus was at the Last Supper and predicting that He was going to have to die soon, He told his disciples, "A new command I give you: Love one another. As I have loved you, so you must love one another. By this everyone will know that you are my disciples, if you love one another" (John 13:34-35). The bond and love between believers is so strong and so unnatural to the rest of the world that even strangers can tell that we follow Jesus just by how we love each other! Love your brothers and sisters in Christ with an *agape* type of love. *Agape* is the type of love that God gives us, and it is an unconditional and selfless love. Do your best to be at peace with your brothers and sisters so that there won't be any divisions in the Church that keep us from being united.

Unity can be difficult because it involves denying ourselves in order to meet the needs of other people, but this generation needs to be united for a common cause. If we all have a purpose that we feel called to, we'll be a whole lot stronger than if we were all striving for different things. The way Christ brings people together is incredible, so find unity in the body of Christ.

Mentorships

As I said, God never intended us to live a life on our own and without guidance. Jesus *is* the Wonderful Counselor, but sometimes He speaks through other people in order to speak into your life. If you want to go into the world in order to do important things for God's Kingdom, you need people who are going to guide you and encourage you. Never be afraid to ask for help from other people because you might feel as though you should be able to handle all of your problems on your own. It's important to have other people who have a life of faith that you can look up to and try to emulate.

Start to pray that the Lord would bring mentors and leaders into your life in order to guide you. You may find leadership in your parents, in people at your church, or even from teachers in your school. Once you find someone you would like to mentor you, ask them if they would regularly meet with you to talk about your walk with God. Always be transparent with your mentors so that they can give you good advice and guide you through your teenager years.

Not only should you have mentors to lead you who are older and more experienced than you, but you also need people your age to support you and push you to be the very best person you can be. When you have friends who also have the mind of Christ, you will be inspired to continue to grow in your faith. For a lot of us teenagers, we might act differently around our friends than we would act around the leaders of our church or with our parents. We need to be the same people whether we're at church or at school, and we can't change the type of person we are depending on who we hang out with. This generation needs to learn how to be Christlike at all times and around all people. If you have friends who are strong Christ followers and who hold you accountable, it will be much easier to be the same person no matter where you are.

Finding people to mentor you and stand by your side is an important part of being unified as the body of Christ. Hanging around other world changers is a great way to stay inspired and passionate about the work of the Lord. Make friendships with your brothers and sisters in Christ because these will be the best relationships that you'll find in life. Relationships within the Church are important because we need other Christians to lift us up and support us. When you are rooted in the body of Christ you'll never have to face anything alone.

CHAPTER 7

Find a Passion

I believe that there's a difference between our purpose and our calling. Our *purpose* is to live to bring glory to God in everything we do. Our purpose is to love God and to learn to be more like Christ for all the days of our lives. Our *calling* is something more specific within our purpose. To put it in different words, your calling is what you're supposed to "do with your life." I've been talking about "being called" to this generation, and I think that we're all called to serve our own generation, but there may be something else that you want to pursue that represents a calling in your life. Just as the world needs Christians in every profession, the world also needs Christians who have different callings. If we were all called to help children in Africa, where would the people be to evangelize to people of other religions or to help out the homeless? Every calling is uniquely beautiful and important to God's Kingdom.

In the right time, God will reveal to you what your calling is. He may speak to you audibly and tell you where He wants you to go, or it could be a quiet whisper in your heart. What I've found when I don't know whether it's God speaking to me or if it's my own voice is that if the thought keeps nagging me and I can't seem to shake it off until I do something about it, then it's probably from God. Also, whatever you're hearing in your heart must line up with the Word of God. If you think God is telling you to stay in your basement and play video games all day, then I would probably assume that feeling isn't from God; but hey, you never know.

As Christians we are told to go to all nations and tell people about Jesus. If you ever feel completely lost as to what you're supposed to do in your life, Matthew 28:19-20 says, "Therefore go and make disciples of all nations, baptizing them in the name of the Father and of the Son and of the Holy Spirit, and teaching them to obey everything I have commanded you," and that verse would be a great place to start when you're looking for your calling.

No calling is more important than another, so if you feel like you aren't as Godly because you're not being called to something that seems significant, don't worry.

You may not think that what you're supposed to do is going to be important, but it will be. You don't have to try to fake a passion for something you really don't feel called to just because you think it's the *right* thing to do. Another thing is that when Jesus says to go to "all nations," that includes your own country and even your own city. You don't have to go halfway around the world to find your calling (though that may be the place you're supposed to go), because you are needed right where you are.

God put you in the place you're in for a very specific reason, so don't get too lost in dreams of the future when you can serve God from right where you are. A lot of people just wish they could leave home and go find their calling, but part of being able to fulfill your calling is being right in God's timing. If you're supposed to go somewhere else than where you are right now, you *will* get there. If God promised it to you then it will happen, but it will be in God's timing and not yours. It's great that you're so passionate and want to go right now, but don't forget that we need to serve God absolutely anywhere.

Maybe you have no idea what you want to do and you haven't started thinking about the future at all because you think you're too young to decide or that you have a lot of time. Time is always short even if you're young because the writer of Psalms says to God, "You have made my days a mere hand-breadth; the span of my years is as nothing before [Y]ou" (Psalm 39:5). Time may seem to drag along slowly, but our days are numbered and the time for action is now. Don't wait until you're older to find your calling because you can live in your calling right now! God is ultimately the one who will tell you what your calling is, but there's no harm in thinking about what you want to do.

If you want to start searching for your calling, first think about what things in your life that you have struggled with. Have you battled depression, self-harm, an eating disorder, or low self-esteem? Have you ever doubted God or not believed in Him? Have you been abused, abandoned, or have you experienced a horrible tragedy? Have you been radically saved by Jesus from a life of terrible sin? Have your parents been through a divorce? Have you fought a sickness? Begin to think about what experiences have shaped you into the person you are today. God wants to take the things you've struggled with, turn them into something good, and use them to help other people.

Don't let a difficulty pass without letting God make it a blessing in your life and in the lives of other people. Sometimes God lets hard times happen to let you grow and to give you experience to be able to help others who may be facing the same thing. Looking back on your life might be the place where you find your calling as you realize that you have a heart for people who are facing the same things you did.

Something else to think about when searching for your calling is what breaks your heart. Is it starving children, people who don't know the truth about God, people who have depression, people with eating disorders, those in poverty, people in other countries, the homeless, orphans, widows, people of other religions, atheists, the elderly, the imprisoned, the disabled, children, those with low self-esteem, the fatherless, gang members, the abused, the juvenile delinquents, the addicts, the least of these, the sick, street kids, or your city? Whatever or whoever you feel called to serve, serve with all your heart. Show the world the light of Jesus.

We first must have a radical passion for Jesus Christ Himself if we hope to see change in our world. If we aren't filled with Christ's love, how could we give His love to others? Trying to pour out His love without being filled with it would be like trying to pour water out of an empty bucket. Just as we all have different talents that create unity in the body, finding our different passions and pursuing them as our calling will also form something that is unstoppable. Find something that you are passionate about in addition to Jesus and our generation. What type of life is a life lived without passion?

What you're passionate about may be the place that Jesus calls you. Find a place where you love to serve and shine Christ's light through your passion.

CHAPTER 8

Achievements

Our generation is far too satisfied with being ordinary. All we want is to stay inside of the mold that other people have created for us because we're afraid that if we step out, people will look at us differently. Maybe you say you want to be different than everyone else, but haven't you really conformed to the society around you? How do you dress? How do you talk to other people? What do you like to do for fun? Are you a carbon copy of all of the other teenagers in our generation? Obviously there are going to be things in your life that are similar to other teenagers because we're all growing up together, but is your *character* different than other people? Are you fed up with the status quo? If you ever hope to be used by God, you cannot accept or conform to the ways of the world, just like Romans 12:2 says: "Do not conform to the pattern of this world, but be transformed by the renewing of your mind."

If Jesus has touched your life, begin to pursue the things of God. Start praying and dreaming of the great things you would like to see the Lord do through your life. As hard as it will be at first, try to seek the Lord's will in what He wants you to do. A simple prayer I use a lot is, "Lord, please use me. I have no idea how You're going to, but I pray You would use me to make a difference for You." By being open to God, there's a lot less room to go in a direction of your *own* choosing rather than God's. Be encouraged by the fact that you can never out-dream God because He is so big! The more you get to know the Lord and the more you give your life to Him, the more your dreams will start to change.

As you grow in Christ, you may not necessarily believe in the importance of striving for the "American Dream" anymore, but you'll realize that in Christ, you're free to have dreams that are even bigger than the "American Dream." The Bible says that "in all your ways submit to [H]im, and [H]e will make your paths straight" (Proverbs 3:6), so commit your dreams into the Lord's hands and He will make them come to fruition. Pray for a heart that holds God's desires rather than your own, because goals that don't match up with God's plan and don't give Him glory probably won't end up happening. Sometimes it's hard to give up a dream that you've held onto for a long time and entrust it to the Lord, but His intimate love and concern will guard that dream until the time is right for you to attain it. Dream God-sized dreams, and He will bring you God-sized achievements.

Now we're ready to actually talk about the "big things" that we've been vaguely referring to up until this point. As you begin to be faithful in the little things that God calls you to do, whether that's reading your Bible every day or sweeping the floors at your church, the Lord will start to call you into bigger roles. If you are unsure of what "big things" for God even look like, I want to give you some ideas you can begin to dream about to pursue for God's glory. All of your dreams and goals should be for the purpose of bringing glory to God. There is no glory for *me* in the equation of following Jesus.

Start thinking nationally, globally, and generationally. Dream *huge* dreams. God isn't turned off by the size of your goals, because nothing is too hard for Him. God is "able to do immeasurably more than all we ask or imagine, according to his power that is at work within us" (Ephesians 3:20), so *dream*. If you want to do important things for God's Kingdom, though, you have to turn those dreams into action. Do you want to see your school saved and be the leader of a movement?

Find other Christians who go to your school, start a Bible study, live your life differently than other kids, and start telling people about Jesus.

Do you have a passion for music and worship? Start practicing and get involved in a church or program that will help you grow into being a worship leader. If you have a big dream, don't expect God to place you into the huge role right away. He wants you to be faithful in making the steps that it takes in order to reach a dream. If you feel like you're too important to do the little things that won't get a lot of attention from other people, you probably aren't ready to step into the spotlight.

Yes, God is the one who does everything, but you still need to take action! If the action you take isn't the right way to go, the Lord will close doors, make it obvious that you're going the wrong direction, help you go the right way instead, and call it a lesson learned. As I pointed out earlier, prayer is where everything begins, so start to pray for the right way to go. When you know what you're supposed to do, take action. We cannot be a generation of people who *wait,* but a generation of people who actually *do something*!

What's the point of being a Christian if you never even have dreams that you want to accomplish for God's glory? If all you want is to have a convenient life, enough money, and to stay within your comfort zone, why do you even need God at all? You can live the "American Dream" completely on your own. We need to be a generation of people who have such huge dreams and who want to do so much for God's Kingdom that we can't even accomplish anything without the Lord because we are too small to do it alone!

Start thinking bigger than just having a life of going to college, finding a good job, getting married, and having a family just because that's all you've ever thought you'd do with your life. Don't get me wrong, the living I just described is a great achievement that many do not have the privilege of reaching, but even within the "American Dream" you can *still* be a radical world changer who is passionate about God's Kingdom. No matter what type of life you and your family live, I promise there is *more* out there for you. I refuse to live a normal, teenage life because I know that God has called me to something greater than just average, and I know that He has called you too.

As scary as it sounds, try to think outside the mold of what our generation considers success. In our teenage years, a successful life is one that consists of cool parents, crazy parties, the hottest clothes, an exciting dating life, and the adoration of our peers. I think that most of us view success later in life as having a good time in college, finding a career that makes lots of money, eventually getting married, and then settling down to a big house with a boat for the weekends. In this typical goal, where is there anything about making a difference in someone's life? Where is the thought that our lives shouldn't just revolve around making ourselves happy? Don't you think that there's something *greater*? Most people have a selfish view of the future, but there's way more fulfillment in living for a greater purpose than there is for living to find our own happiness.

You may be thinking that if you can't hope to experience the "American Dream" some day because Jesus is even taking *that* goal away from you, then what type of life can you live? The type of life Jesus wants you to live isn't just a comfortable life; it's a fulfilled life. That life isn't a life filled with riches; it's a life lived in abundance. His type of life doesn't just find happiness; His life finds joy. Jesus came so that we "may have life, and have it to the full" (John 10:10). Jesus doesn't ask you to give up a life of fulfillment. He just asks you to let Him redefine what real fulfillment actually is. A life lived for a higher purpose is one that is filled to the brim with every spiritual *and* every physical need you could ever have.

If you decide that you want to live a life filled with great exploits done for the Lord, then jump into it with both feet. Take action and begin to do the "big things" you've always dreamed of, but this time place a real dream instead of just a vague idea between those quotation marks. Define what you want your "big things" to be and start doing what you have to do in order to achieve those dreams the Lord has put in your heart. Put everything into God's hands because He will take your goals and do more with them than you would ever be able to do on your own.

On your own you may be able to accomplish things the world views as great, but they probably won't be for God's glory if you only do them by your own power. God can take even the simplest goal and turn it into something huge that could change a generation. Jesus even said, "Very truly I tell you, whoever believes in me will do the works I have been doing, and they will do even greater things than these, because I am going to the Father" (John 14:12). Enjoy reading the Gospels to see all the amazing things that Jesus did and to be set on fire by the fact that we can do *even greater things*. Let's be a generation of people who have big actions to go along with our big dreams.

Whatever you love to do, whatever you're passionate about, whatever you're good at, work at it with all your heart and do it for God's glory. No matter how small or insignificant something you love may seem, if you take what you do and give it over to God He can do something great with it. If you play sports, always give the glory to God for the ability He's given you to play. If you are in the arts, create things to show Jesus' light to people. If you like to volunteer, don't just serve to make other people see how *good* you are; point everything back to God.

If you feel as though you are someone who doesn't have a *great* talent that you could express for God's glory (you just haven't found your gifting yet, because you do have talents), then learn to be Christlike in every thought, word, and deed. I cannot stress enough that we need a generation of people who strive to be high achievers for God. Strive for excellence in what you do, and I promise that God will honor your efforts and turn them into something great that He can use to reach this generation through you.

PART 3

Get in the Game

CHAPTER 9

The World Is Watching

A blessing and a curse that come along with being a teenager is that we are always under the watchful eye of the adults around us. I believe that of all the generations living on Earth right now, ours is the one which most people are watching in order to see what we do next. Essentially, we are the ones who run the world. Maybe we aren't the ones who are literally *in charge*, but the future of the world rests on our shoulders. Businesses market mainly to teenagers because whatever we consider "cool" is what they want to sell, so that means that we have *a lot* of power. The world is essentially in our hands, so we need to use it to our advantage.

We have a lot of influence on the world around us, and especially on the generations that come after us.

Have you noticed that the kids who are younger than us are growing up with all of the modern technologies that we've really just become accustomed to ourselves? Kids have iPhones, Facebook accounts, and they say things that teenagers shouldn't even be saying! We laugh about being "'90s kids" who had better lives than the kids today, but hasn't our culture rubbed off on the generation after us? Their behavior had to be learned from somewhere, didn't it?

It's no wonder that little kids act like teenagers, because we're the people that they look up to! What kind of example are we setting for the future generations? We're a culture of people constantly being fed by a harmful media that encourages us to act in ways that aren't Christlike, and we wonder why people look down on us. It's time for this generation to take a stand and take responsibility for its actions. You're going to leave behind a legacy, positive or negative, that hundreds of years from now people will be talking about.

Not only do we need to be leaders that future generations can look up to, but we have to be people that even the rest of the world admires. When the apostle Paul wrote a letter to a younger believer named Timothy, Paul told him, "Don't let anyone look down on you because you are young, but set an example for the believers in speech, in conduct, in love, in faith and in purity" (1 Timothy 4:12). This verse means that not only are we role models for those who are younger than us, but we're even leaders to people who are *older* than us. Maybe if our generation stood up to lead the world for Christ, then our own leaders would be convicted to examine the way that they live. We can have an impact that is *multigenerational*, and that is an exciting opportunity.

Start living in a way that will make people stop and wonder what's happening in our generation. If we got out of God's way, stopped resisting Him, and let Him move over our generation, the world couldn't help but notice. What if we stopped supporting organizations that wanted to erase Christianity from the world? What if we stood up and made it our declaration to refuse the standards that the world sets, but live within the standards that Jesus sets for us? If teenagers like us began a revolution for the name of Jesus, we would be the talk of not just the town, but the whole world!

It's always incredible when you see people your own age starting groups for a cause that they're passionate about, but you don't just have to watch anymore; you could start something too. When I say "something," I mean that you could start a charity, you could lead a Bible study, you could start a movement of teenagers living for Christ—the possibilities are endless. All you have to do is rise up to the call that the Lord has placed on your life and have the courage to step out in faith.

Jesus says to, "Let your light shine before others, that they may see your good deeds and glorify your Father in heaven" (Matthew 5:16). Don't be afraid to let Christ's light shine because there is no shame in living the Gospel. If you're afraid of what people would think if you stepped out to live a life for Christ, then get other people to step out with you so that you are all stronger together! The more people that start to rise up to take the world for Jesus, the more support you'll have around you to do great things for God's glory.

For all the men of God reading this, I think part of the problem that our generation is facing is that there aren't enough men to step up and be leaders. Too many of you are either too afraid to stand up for Christ because you're worried about what your friends might think or you have other priorities that you've put before your walk with God. Following Jesus is your number one priority and everything else comes second to Him. The more time you spend learning about God and getting to know Him as your Lord, the more Christlike you will become and in turn you will become a better leader, because Jesus was the ultimate leader. Stand up and lead, men of God! A huge part of whether this generation rises up to change the world rests on your choice of whether or not you're *all in* for Christ.

I sometimes think that guys are even more self-conscious than girls because a lot of you are afraid to stand up to your friends and do the right thing. I encourage you to ask yourself what's really important: winning temporary popularity, or winning souls for an eternity with Christ. Refuse to live by the standards that the world lives by and say "no" to ungodliness and impurity: "But you, man of God, flee from all this [sin], and pursue righteousness, godliness, faith, love, endurance, and gentleness" (1 Timothy 6:11). Be a true disciple of Jesus Christ and make the world wonder what's happening in the hearts of the teenage boys of our generation.

For all you women of God, refuse to let the world shape you into what it wants you to be. Be a woman of love, tenderness, purity, and godliness. The world wants nothing more than for you to be impure and give yourself away into darkness, but don't let the evil get a hold on your heart. The world wants to bind you into believing that you aren't good enough the way God created you so that it can make you do what it says it takes to be loved and popular. The world will tell you that you aren't really a woman if you don't have a boyfriend, and that you need to give up your purity if you ever hope to get a man to love you. It will tell you that a life of godliness is boring and old-fashioned.

As women of God, we have to protect ourselves from every lie that the enemy tells us or we'll start to actually *believe* what he says. All the ways that the world tries to shape you will tear you away from God, so guard your heart. I pray that the Lord would protect you from the ways of this world, but you have to *want* to let Jesus protect you or else none of His attempts to guard you will work. If you keep testing the waters to see just how far you can go without completely giving in to the world, you're building up walls that keep you from God.

Keep your heart as protected from the world as possible. Pray that the Lord would guard your heart at all times, because even if you aren't looking for trouble, it may still come your way when you least expect it. The world is in a fight to take your heart from God and this isn't a joke; this is serious business! You're not going to win every battle that the world throws at you, but what matters is that you let the Lord win the war for your heart.

Girls, I encourage you to protect yourselves from the world as much as possible so that you can grow into strong women of God who do great things for the Lord. The more you're surrounded by God, the less the world can take you from your calling to rise up and take a stand for our generation. Refuse to live as a woman of the world and instead say "no" to everything that isn't of the Lord. "What, then, shall we say in response to these things? If God is for us, who can be against us?" (Romans 8:31). Let's rise up and make the world stop to see what God is doing in our hearts.

Our generation needs to realize how much of an impact we have on the rest of the world. Time is running low for us because soon we'll be old news and the younger kids will take our place. If we stand up and start to move in Jesus' direction, there's no way that the rest of the world *isn't* going to notice. The media may try to hide what God is doing in our hearts, but just as Jesus said, "A town built on a hill cannot be hidden" (Matthew 5:14). The world is watching our every move, so let's give them something that's actually worth Tweeting, Facebooking, and blogging about.

CHAPTER 10

What Is It That's Stopping Us?

You might be asking, "Well then, what's stopping us from being leaders if our generation is so important?" Unfortunately right now, I believe that a lot of things are stopping us from reaching our full potential, but I still have faith that God is going to do a work in us. The author of Psalms says to God that "even the darkness will not be dark to [Y]ou; the night will shine like the day, for the darkness is as light to [Y]ou" (Psalm 139:12). Yes, there is a lot of darkness that hovers over our generation, but God's light is so great that He can pierce through any evil with the greatest of ease.

You may also be wondering why God hasn't done anything to change our generation if He has the power to do so. My answer to this question is that God is waiting on *us* to make the next move. The Lord has given us everything we need in order to see change in our generation—whether our needs are resources, leaders, or passions—but we just don't know that we have all of this wealth waiting to be unleashed.

I think that one of the biggest things that our enemy, Satan, uses against God's people is fear that stops us from taking action. There are an endless amount of worries that you could have about taking a stand for the Gospel, and if you're anything like me, pretty much all of those fears go through your head on a daily basis. Maybe you fear that you'll lose friends or that your family will shun you if you step up for your faith.

Maybe you don't trust God enough to realize that He'll guide every one of your steps even if you don't know what's to come in your walk with Him, and so you fear the unknown. Maybe you're worried that God is going to abandon you in a great time of need or that He'll ask you to do something that's too far outside of your comfort zone. Maybe you're even afraid that if you radically give your life over to Christ that you won't see change in anyone's life and it'll all have been a waste.

First off, God cares about every concern that you have. He doesn't dismiss your worries and count you off as unholy because you're afraid. Even Jesus was afraid to die on the cross! I encourage you to turn your fears over to the Lord. First Peter 5:7 says, "Cast all your anxiety on [H]im because [H]e cares for you." If you've put your trust in Jesus as your Savior and turned to live your life for Jesus in order to receive His grace of an eternity in Heaven, then your future is secure. No matter what happens in your life or what God asks you to do, you have the ultimate hope of living with Jesus forever and so you don't have anything to fear. Jesus wants you to turn your fear over to Him because fear is of the enemy. Because God promises in His Word that He is always with you, you have nothing to be afraid of. Rely on Jesus for every need you have, especially your worry, because He will carry you through.

Another thing that stops us from living our lives for Christ is our selfish nature. Because our flesh is so sinful, it is most natural for us to go into survival mode and only think of ourselves. As Christians, though, there is so much more for us that waits right outside our selfishness. Take a step outside yourself and start to look around at the needs of others, because there truly is great need.

Yes, there are people everywhere who need basic physical essentials, but the greatest need in our world is first and foremost the need for Christ. Not only do people need Jesus so that they can receive an eternity in Heaven, but people also need Jesus just to be able to get through their days. Can you imagine your life without Jesus? When you get to know Jesus more and more intimately, you'll realize how much you depend on Him and you'll start to notice just how many people haven't found that they can rely on Him too.

As you learn more about who Jesus is, you'll start to see that He was the most selfless person who ever existed. The Bible says that when you realize exactly how selfless Jesus was, then you will learn how to, "Do nothing out of selfish ambition or vain conceit. Rather, in humility value others above yourselves, not looking to your own interests but each of you to the interests of others" (Philippians 2:3-4).

Not only should we be selfless so that we can help other people, but we also need to be selfless so that we can be used by God! If we're too concerned with our own desires, God can't show us what His desires are for our lives. If we stay within our selfish nature, we probably won't recognize the opportunities God gives us to serve our generation because we'll be too focused on ourselves. Humble yourself and start to ask God to break down your selfishness and pride. It's a long process for God to remove our negative qualities because they are dug so deeply in our hearts, but, "Is anything too hard for the Lord?" (Genesis 18:14).

Finally, I think the last main thing that keeps us from our purpose is not knowing that we have one. We have to realize that we have a higher calling than just to find happiness for ourselves. I think a lot of teenagers don't understand that there's something *more* to this life than just having fun and being distracted by everything around us. Maybe you've tried to get your life right before God but it seems like you were pulled away in the next moment because of all the distractions in the world. The enemy uses things that were created by God, such as friends, relationships, school, and family, and twists those things into distractions that keep us from our purpose. So even if you understand that you have a purpose, you're going to face the distractions of the world.

Let me first say that distractions are everywhere and will never completely go away, but you can learn how to deal with them. Sometimes things that get in our way are from the enemy, but sometimes God puts things in our path to redirect us or point us back to Him. Whatever interruptions you face in your walk with God, always remember that the Lord is your absolute priority and that you need to go to Him with everything. The less you dwell on your distractions, the less those distractions will affect you. There are also steps you can take in order to limit the amount of interferences that you see in your life, such as separating yourself from the world as much as possible. Just because you face a setback doesn't mean that your purpose has become void. Just get back up and try again, and the Lord will bless your struggle.

There are a lot more than just these three things that hold our generation back from the high calling that we have, so I would encourage you to spend time seeking what most holds *you* back. When in doubt, turn to prayer and remember that you are a chosen child of God who has a purpose in your generation. When our generation starts to recognize our weaknesses and the things that keep us from God, we will know what we're fighting against and be able to stand up to it in the name of Jesus. Let's be a generation of teenagers who stand up to what wants to tear us down and refuse to let the world stop us.

CHAPTER 11

The Testimony of a Generation

There are a lot of things that we can do as a generation to leave a lasting legacy, but I believe the most important mind-set to leave behind for others to follow is one of purity. To be someone who strives for purity is exceedingly rare in our society today because hardly anyone even believes that purity is important. Being pure is an amazing, but extremely overlooked, way to set yourself apart for God's glory. Because so many people live impure lives, being a person who is pure automatically makes you different from the rest of the world.

When I talk about purity I'm not just referring to abstinence; purity is so much more than just waiting until marriage to have sex. Purity is a way of life that shows the world that you follow a Holy God. According to Dictionary.com, the word "pure" means, "free from anything of a different, inferior, or contaminating kind." Being pure means that you keep the things of the world from contaminating you so that you can seek God without any hindrances, and Hebrews 12:1 tells us to "throw off everything that hinders." Just as a woman wears a white wedding dress on her wedding day, so the Bride of Christ needs to be clothed in white purity that honors God.

Maybe you've never known that there was purity apart from the physical purity of our bodies, but your entire life can be pure. Waiting until marriage to have sex is already a great testimony because most people believe abstinence is old-fashioned, but having your entire life be pure is even better. You can be pure in your thoughts, in your words, and in your motivations. Pursuing purity is another way to strive to be Christlike because Jesus was completely holy in every way. Jesus never had an impure thought or even said an impure word, and the more we grow to be like Christ, the more pure we will become.

Having a pure heart will manifest itself through a life of purity, so pray for the purification of your heart. The psalmist David prayed, "Create in me a pure heart, O God" (Psalm 51:10) after he had committed adultery, so you're never *too* far gone to ask God to purify you! When your heart is pure, you are going to live a pure life, and just as Paul wrote to another Christian named Titus, "To the pure, all things are pure" (Titus 1:15).

So how do we live pure lives? First, we have to ask God to cleanse us. If you want to live a life of purity, Jesus' blood can wipe away every stain that's been on your heart. Sometimes, the purification process is extremely painful because we have to dig deep and realize how black our hearts are, but Jesus will heal you of any darkness. Next, we have to start pursuing purity. Maybe there are books or magazines that you read that you need to get rid of. Maybe there are movies that you need to stop watching and music that you need to stop listening to because they cause impure thoughts. Maybe you even have relationships that compromise your purity that you need to separate yourself from.

Whatever it is, nothing is as important as the purity of your heart, so don't be afraid to get rid of anything. Another way to strive for purity is to make sure that you stay away from situations that would cause you to stray from your pure life. If it causes you to stumble even just a little bit, it probably needs to go.

There are temptations everywhere, but the Holy Spirit is powerful enough to guard your heart and mind in all situations. A verse that is very encouraging to me says, "No temptation has overtaken you except what is common to mankind. And God is faithful; [H]e will not let you be tempted beyond what you can bear. But when you are tempted, [H]e will also provide a way out so that you can endure it" (1 Corinthians 10:13). So any time you find yourself in a situation where you are tempted by impurity, God is right there with you, ready to help you overcome the temptation. Don't even put yourself in situations where you know there will be temptation because sin is waiting to trap you and make you stumble; just stay away from it completely.

Pursue the things of God rather than the things of this world and you will find yourself becoming more and more pure. Fill yourself with the Word of God and there won't be any room for impurity. The more you read your Bible, listen to worship music and sermons, and fill yourself up with things that are from God, you'll find that your life will begin to exude purity and godliness. Seek God above everything else, and He will make you more like Himself.

Because we live in such an impure world, we need God more than ever in order to help us guard our hearts. It used to be true that you would have to go *looking* to find sin, but now sin is just a click away on the computer or a channel away on the TV. If you recognize that impurity is lurking around every corner, it will be much easier to stay away from it because it won't take you by surprise. There's a difference between being naïve and being pure, so knowing that impurity is out there won't compromise your pure heart, but actually help you in the fight against pollution.

Because we're all sinners, we all come from a past of impurity. Maybe you think that you can't ever be pure because of the way you used to live your life before you knew Jesus. One of the most beautiful things about Jesus is that He can wash away *all* of your sin and make you whole again. God says that, "'Though your sins are like scarlet, they shall be as white as snow'" (Isaiah 1:18). No matter what type of life you have lived, Jesus longs to give you a new start. Live in the freedom that comes from repentance!

A major trap of the enemy is to keep God's people living in the condemnation of their past, but know that Jesus' death on the cross has paid the penalty for all of our sins. Maybe you've started to live a life of purity but impure thoughts always seem to be your natural reaction because of the way you used to live. Take heart, because the Lord can even change the way you think so that your first reaction is one of purity. Keep pursuing God and His holiness and He will make you as white as snow.

This world has completely lost the passion for purity, so let's be the generation that brings the fire back. Live a life of complete purity so that you can show Jesus to the world. Because being pure is so diffi-cult, you will learn how much you need to rely on Jesus in order to help you live a pure life. You're only human, so you're going to fail at times, but don't beat yourself up too much. Just keep going in the direction of purity and over time you'll grow to be more and more sanctified. Never forget how powerful a life of purity is in showing people that you live for God. Show the world that purity isn't something to stay away from, but that it's something to run to.

CHAPTER 12

The Time Is Now

In the Old Testament, a woman named Esther was made queen because the king of the land thought she was very beautiful. A time came when the king wanted to destroy all the Israelites, and Esther, being an Israelite herself, was their only hope to get the king to change his mind. Esther's uncle, Mordecai, told her that she needed to go to the king in order to save her people, but Esther was afraid. Mordecai was trying to encourage Esther to stand up to the king and so he asked her, "'And who knows but that you have come to your royal position for such a time as this?'" (Esther 4:14). Mordecai was trying to tell Esther that God had placed her in the position of queen because she was called to save the Israelites. Esther was called "for such a time as this."

Our stories may be different than Esther's, but we're all in the same position. We are all called for such a time as this. You are *not* too young to be a warrior for Christ. If you're reading this book, no matter how young or how old you are, you can do something for God's Kingdom. The Bible is full of stories of God calling out young people to do His work, and most of the heroes in the Word were younger than we would expect when we look at the feats they accomplished.

A great example of a young person being called is the story of David and Goliath. The Bible says that when David stood before Goliath, the giant "looked David over and saw that he was little more than a boy" (1 Samuel 17:42). David may have been little, but he was *bold*. David told Goliath, "You come against me with sword and spear and javelin, but I come against you in the name of the Lord Almighty, the God of the armies of Israel, whom you have defied. This day the Lord will deliver you into my hands" (1 Samuel 17:45-46). Just look at David's faith! He was so confident that God would give him the victory that he didn't even wear any armor to fight a giant that was more than nine feet tall.

Maybe you don't have to face a literal giant, but what are the Goliaths in your life? What is it that you have to stand up against and have faith that God will deliver you from? Have the amount of faith David did when you fight your biggest obstacles. During one of the biggest tests of his life when he stood up against Goliath, David didn't doubt for one second that God would fail him, but do *you* have the same confidence?

If you continue to seek the Lord and His calling for your life, there will come a time when He will call you to a task that is impossible without His help, but those are the responsibilities that do the greatest work for His Kingdom. If you want to do big things for God He *will* honor your desire, but it isn't always going to be easy. Actually, it will rarely be easy at all. But how rewarding would it be to do something in your own power when the God of the universe wants to increase the effect you can have tenfold?

The time is *now*, so be ready. God is searching for those who are prepared to be called into something great and He wants to use you! Don't ever think that you are too young to do big things for God's Kingdom because He desires to use young people. If God always used people who were experienced and qualified, the miracles wouldn't seem as great to the rest of the world because people would just think that the person God used was doing everything in their own power. If the Lord used a young person, though—someone who the world would never expect to do something great— God would get a whole lot more of the glory because it would be obvious that He *had* to have been involved.

The Lord wants to call you into greater roles, so prepare your heart and remember that all of the honor is His.

A quote that I've heard people repeat a lot is, "God doesn't call the qualified, but He qualifies the called," so maybe you feel like you don't have enough experience or talent to be used by God. Let me tell you right now that you are *not* too inexperienced for God to work through you. God can use anyone He wants whose heart is turned toward Him. All the Lord wants to see is a willing heart to go where He calls. You don't have to have a ton of experience because God will provide all of the resources that you need. Don't let the excuse that you aren't good enough hold you back from the huge calling that the Lord has on your life. Be encouraged that God wants to use you just the way you are! The more human you are, the more room that God has to bring glory to Himself, which is always the goal.

Don't let the enemy lie to you and say that you can't be used by God, because you were called for such a time as this! There are all sorts of things he will try to tell you that will keep you from experiencing all that the Lord has for you. A common lie is the thought that you've messed up too many times for God to ever use you. Maybe you feel as though you aren't worthy of letting God shine through you. The fact is that none of us are worthy of God using us for His Kingdom, but for some crazy reason He still uses us anyway.

View your past as a greater testimony to what God can do in a person's life. I think that a lot of people want to hear a more personal view of God and what He's accomplished in your life rather than just rattling off facts about Him. Of course, knowing about God is crucial, but your testimony is just as powerful. Tell people how God has changed you at every opportunity you get because you never know what your story could spark in another person. They may hear the way that God has saved you and desire that for themselves too.

The times are desperate, so we can't wait another minute to let God shine through us. We need to quit putting things off into the tomorrow that never actually comes. Today is the day that we need to stand boldly for our generation.

Stop waiting because the time is now! You are not *too young*, you are not *too inexperienced*, and you are not *too unimportant*. God wants to use you right now in your youth, so don't be afraid to let Him.

Closing Remarks

My prayer for you is that this book has been a journey that God uses in your life to get you to reach your full potential. We've traveled through getting your life right before Jesus, beginning to prepare your heart in order to start doing big things, and finally, the implications of God working through us. The enemy wants to hold you back from what God is going to do through you, so I pray in Jesus' name for His hand of protection on your life. You will be attacked by the devil because you're becoming more and more important to God's Kingdom and Satan does not like that. Doubts are going to creep in, but when they do, always go to the source of our hope, Jesus Christ.

If God takes you through seasons that are really difficult and you feel like you're drifting away from the Lord, start at the beginning and examine your own walk with Him first so that you can find out where the problem is. Let God be constantly pouring His love into you so that you can show His love that overflows from your heart to the world. Pray boldly for the Lord's rich blessing on your life and for an overwhelming change in our generation. Never forget that you have a purpose and an extremely high calling that the Lord has placed on your life. Hold on tightly to the calling that God has given to your life and guard it at all costs. Your life is so important to God's Kingdom! You have been chosen to lead a whole generation.

Be bold and confident, but boast only in God. Stand up and be the brave men and women of God that the Lord has called you to be. When in doubt, always go back to the Lord.

Let's stand up and rise, generation.

www.ingramcontent.com/pod-product-compliance
Lightning Source LLC
Chambersburg PA
CBHW071638050426
42443CB00026B/706